The August Rain

A collection of poetry
by
Stephen Komarnyckyj

KLP
Kalyna Language Press

First published in the UK in 2016 by Kalyna Language Press

Copyright - Stephen Komarnyckyj 2015

All rights reserved. No part of this publication may be reproduced or transmitted in any form or by any means, electronic or mechanical, including photocopy, recording or otherwise without prior permission in writing from the publisher.

ISBN 978-0-9931972-4-6

Acknowledgements

Poems in this book have appeared in *Black and Blue Revolution, Dreamcatcher, Envoi, Fire, Fjords, Frost, Ink, Sweat and Tears, LA Review, London Grip, Modern Poetry in Translation, Poetry Salzburg, Tellus, The Stockholm Review of Literature, The Write Place*, and *Zaporogue*. The Antonych translation was published on the *And Other Stories* site as part of a European Society of Authors initiative to promote neglected European literatures. Duet also appears in *Night Music*, a collection of translations of the work of Bohdan Ihor Antonych, published by Kalyna Language Press following a grant received from English PEN.

Contents

Tickling	1
1915	2
Green	4
You Were	5
For My Father	7
Batko	8
A Song of Exile	10
Peter Sutcliffe	15
Your Shout	16
Bull	18
I Dreamed, Love	19
Whitby	20
My Cat and Crazy Rainbows	24
Vasya's Biggest Secret	25
There Are Mirrors	26
Lenin Takes a Dip	28
Khersonesos	30
Pavlo's Lament	31
Cathedral	33
Nowhere	34
I Dreamed	36
Something Fishy	37
This Is	38
Out of the Belfry	39
Too Late	41
Wharncliffe	43
I Did Not Know	45
Vasya's Surprise	47
Monet	50
What?	53
A Quail Flies Over the Steppe	55
The Zone	56

August Moon   59
From Edinburgh   60
I Loved to Walk Around the Cages at Night   63
A Letter From Crimea   65

Translations

The Lustre of Surfaces - Volodymyr Svidzinskyi   67

Duet - Bohdan Ihor Antonych   70

Tickling

My father, with his trousers rolled up to his knee,
Stood in the beck, in peat-stained water
That was the gold orange of a delicate tea,
Though curious frills of lace and snow
Bloomed over the stones nearby
And his feet were either bronze or ivory.

It was not those that took me, but his face,
The face of a young man glazed with sunlight,
Stooped over the stream, his gaze
At once enraptured and predatory
And then the trout quite still in his hand.
In dreams he shows me, there is no sound

As he lowers the trout back into the water.
We watch it flex, balance and float,
Curved to a Circassian dagger
Thrust in the river's throat,
And the sand and stones of the river bed
And the water rusted as old blood.

1915

I

By the light of the kerosene lamp,
My grandmother, a little girl,
Kneels like a willow
To say her prayers.
Shadows settle in the thatch
As she whispers

Otche nash. The wind lolls in the firs
That sway on the mountain side,
Hypnotised.
The river slips
Through the earth, a groom
Sinks into his bride.

It is spring and the rye
Blooms with its gold tide
Under the dusk sky;
The dead
Talk, if they talk, soundlessly.
She lays her head

On her pillow, a little girl
Lies on her bed,
Slender as a willow,
While outside the dead
Pass by,
Pass by soundlessly,

Through wheat,
Through rye.

II

In her sleep she hears

Someone hammer at the door,
A huge
Heart beat, thunder,

Then,

She creeps to where her mother
Lay on her bed
Crying, a wounded bird.

And so the soldiers came,
A black tide
Taking from their home

Mother, farmer and bride.

Green

We were driving through the mist in Magdale
Ghosts flaring in our headlights,
The faces in the trees black
As old blood, my hand on your knee,
The apple that fell soundlessly in the orchard,
They taste best my father said
Its skin still chill with dew and grass,
The sweet tartness on my tongue,
A white horse rears in the headlights,
My aunty scattering salt on tomaten

Stefan, you've hardly eaten,
The sandpaper rasp of her voice
Scraping my skin,
From somewhere in a concert hall
Where no one else is playing
The thin attenuated scream
Of a cello when my hand slipped,
The birch a smear of chalk, a wisp of steam,
The country, a Rorschach blot
Tendrils of ink clouding the water,

Your breath on the mirror, darling, fades out,
Your hand chill as a fish in mine,
I called but you were gone,
Somewhere beyond plumes
Of sea grass, the soft
Recess of a sand dune.
The rain's kiss on my face
Still soft and warm,
In my hands, your body
Blurred shifts of light among the birches come.

You Were

A siren wails miles away
And echoes across the valley,
The wind booms through the birches.

You smooth your jeans, the fabric
Clings to your thigh.
The sea

Flattens across the harbour at Whitby,
Foxgloves
Sway. You hope they will take

An ocean of purple plumes,
The waves break
In my imagination.

You tell me of the radishes,
Plump and cool in your hands,
The plums,

Dropping noiselessly
Among couch grass,
Summer's tears, its flesh bombs…

Your voice whispers into the mobile
Off the coast of Norway,
I trail my hands among the purples

Of the sea.
You are miles away
I don't want to be here,

Dusk. Signals dissipating into thin air
The indigo
And waves ticking

Off Viking and Finistere.
The flowers that bear you to me
Pale as sea foam,

Your soul, the shock
Of salt on my tongue
Falling away from the moon,

The waves come.

For My Father

When I was a child I dreamed I would walk
Over the rivers and seas in seven-league boots,

Scooping the water, sifting it with my fingers
For the souls of lost children,

But these days it is my father whom I hear most often calling
From among sea spume and spray, the slap

Of water on the jetty.
What does he say,

This small boy in his plus fours
Under the sepia light of an autumn day

In Ukraine in the nineteen twenties?
He looks at me with eyes as dark

As the rift in his heart,
For all he lost;

Boy with the eyes of a man who knew
The taste

Of blood and its cost.

Batko
For Nestor Makhno

You rinse your sabre
In the River Buh,
Watching the rose-coloured tendrils unfurl,
And a smile,
Flickers across your face,
Barely noticing
The screams of a man who dies,
His head resting
On a pillow of knotgrass, camomile
Trymajtes. Summer,

A glass bowl,
The curve of a still
Where you see your face,
The long hair
Sensitively carved nostrils
Suggestive of a violinist,
Distorted, magnified
A mirage over the Steppe
A broken God
Glimpsed at the periphery of sleep.

Paris. Exile.
The backdrops you painted at a studio,
Flowers, grey as ash,
The glow
Of dusk on the Seine.
Did you hear the dead men
In the scream
of an accordion
The lisp of thawed snow

The vibration

Through the struts of the Eiffel tower
Which a certain Pan Doubinsky or Monsieur
As he insisted with a dry laugh,
Assured you were the very image
Of a giraffe.
No one knows how the man who has brought death
Communes with the slain,
The taste of iron
In the glass of Cabernet Sauvignon,
The face

Of a man pillowed
On camomile and knotgrass
Stares at you in the metro
Petals of apple blossom
Snow of silk,
The whip handle
Of your anarchist cock
Slides into Halyna,
Warm as the marshes of Podillya
In summer,

Further still
Waves of Steppe grass
Cranes' nests
Crows
Plashing in the mud
Laugh,
The sabre slides through flesh so easily
A corpse darkens in the rye.
The flowers by the roadside
Seem artificial, embroidered …

A Song of Exile

I

The river begins as

                A thread of water clinging
                To sandstones and clay.
                It burbles childishly,
                Content to reflect
                The sides of the gully,

Frolics down the altitude
Of moor into the valley,
Water stained the colour
Of old blood, until at last

                The trees smear themselves into place.
                Snot-coloured moss.
                The birch, a smudge of chalk.
                Javelins of couch grass.

Over each weir
Its waters nervously simper,
Moving, yet motionless,
Perspex bells,

                They chime
                Into the waft of lace,
                Foam of champagne.
                Yet still

The river descends and falls
Towards the estuary,
A song line of DNA.

II

There is a place just beyond the boundary of the farm,
By fenced-in trees,
Birches
Raising their arms as if in surrender,
At the edge of the wood
Where nettles
And willow-root nod
Languidly, the summer day
Unravels in cirrus clouds,
Transparencies
Quiver,
Blurring the field's watercolour.
It was a part
Of Lincolnshire,
Untouched
Beyond battalions of leeks and peas,
The slenderness
Of young
Deciduous trees.
With a well-muscled oak,
A beech
Perfecting its backstroke,
Against the wind of the North Sea,
They all overlook
This nowhere place,
The heart
Of England, still untouched,
Bindweed and emptiness.

III

I drift down your spine
The way a raft
Of stratus cloud
Drifts down the Pennines,
      Your blond hair,
      An estuary,
      Spills through the Saxon Shore,
You talk in your sleep,
I touch your instep,
Sway over the dead drop
At the edge of England,
      An unseen hand
      Scrawls chalk on the sea,
      Waves whisper
      Maybe,
A gold javelin
Of sunlight pierces your side
The wounds of God
Heal,
I kiss
The South Down of your thighs,
Catch
The ocean's perfume,
A mouthful of wine,
      England's snapped spine,
      The paralysed glow
      Of the horizon,
      Dover's
      Cliffs, a grin
      Flashed towards France or Spain
      Bloodied tracts run dry
      The rain's graffiti,

      Nearby
      Shoals of light coagulate
      And disperse as mercury,
      The further I drift
The country slips
Over the edge of the world
All that you grip
But cannot hold, the heart's lift...
The yearning of the sea
Beyond gravity

As I draw close
To that chance discovery,
The wild rose of the south
In a northern forest
England's dreaming mouth,
Damp with the soft
Rain of ecstasy
Calyx and stamen silk
Cathedral where we pray
Beyond England's bitter
Sacramental blood,
The kiss of sea spray.

IV
You didn't so much see

                                                                    As sense

The water balanced

                                                       Against the lock gate

Brimming with amber

Coloured light
                    And spears of willowroot
Cradling the bronze
Rim of sunset.

Everything you know
                        Converted to a chance
                              Movement of the canal's
Purloined brilliance

Until it seems I merge into
Bulrushes, the dank
Russet glow

Of dusk
                                   And something else.
Swallows poised to migrate
On telegraph wires,

Flight after flight
Leaving its bars,

And falling through us,
Elsewhere
                                        Possibilities we dream,

The mesmerised air.

Peter Sutcliffe

I went to a pub where he drank once,
Without knowing it.
Wiped a moustache of beer
From my upper lip,
Walked the streets where he murdered,
Stepping carefully around piles of dog shit,
Wore the same flares,
Had the same haircut,
Listened to the same crap music,
Held a woman in my arms like he did
In a slow dance,
Went out on the pull...
I hate the bastard of course
Though we both had
Time to kill.

Your Shout

For Kazantip, the lost Kingdom of Love

Faithless throbbing in the concrete
I can't get no sleep,
A forest of arms swayed, I looked up,
Was it Venus or a satellite
Laid in the sky's indigo velvet?
Kazantip
Ekstas you held a constellation in your palm
Five gold suns smiling,

Fingers sifting the air above us,
I can't get no sleep
Anonymous,

We are a coral forest
Arms swing
Pendulum of bone,
Blue stars tattooed on your breast wobbling

My heart beat
A lambeg drum,   labyrinth of skin

I push my way to the door
Opasno dlya Zhyzny

Outside
Shock of cold air   sand whisper
The white horses
Of the tide rear

I ride them

Harness of foam
Flip back and crucify myself   as the Black Sea slides
Easy as a lover fucking
Ukraine's coastal shelf   vomits me up.

Kazantip,

Your voice wheels over me
Yeb tvoyu Mat!

I throw myself back
Into a sea that seems absurdly black
And cream, milk stout,

God, right now I could drink the world,
Let me die for this pint, though it's your shout.

Bull

If I think of my dad, what I see
Is the grainy image
Extracted from a childhood memory,
A field in Ballymena

Beneath well-muscled grey sky,
A bull bowing to my father
With a strange bovine courtesy
And here is my father

Dancing with the aforementioned bull,
Tussocks springing beneath his feet
Thin and pliant and graceful,
His flexing silhouette

Seems to float on the air
And effortlessly
Elude danger,
Supple as fire

And even now I wonder if I might
Chance upon my father
Dancing with a bull at twilight
And although I'd rather

He was alive I think of this:
His body not quite caught
On the horns and the chance kiss
Of death that left his face

With a kind of tired loveliness.

I Dreamed, Love

I dreamed, love, that the goddesses
Compelled me, like Paris, to choose
Who among them was the fairest
And they paraded before me in the forest,
And as I balanced the apple in my hand
I saw that they all had your face,
And they became as shapes traced in sand
Strewn on a glass through which light plays,
And I knew then I could not choose
For he who would choose betrays,
So, love, forgive my faithlessness,
As I choose not to make a choice,
But find within your wounded heart
The sanctity of the human voice.

Whitby

In honour of Caedmon, the first known English poet

I

A year after our wedding, we walked through
The whalebone arch at Whitby and it seemed
These were our real nuptials under the blue
Nave of sky those weathered ribs had dreamed. Later

You sighed above me in a room
Black as in the belly of a whale,
Your body soft as the meringue of foam
The gale bore up a jetty,

Your voice, the voice of a storm
Warm inlet of the Saxon Shore,
Where the northmen came
And left the treasury of your hair,

Your breast of cloud, your voice the voice
Of the sea pummelling the Yorkshire coast,
The sea's soft incessant noise
As it settles around us with the ghost

Of boats knocking softly at a quay
Ishtar's softness, your alabaster body.

II

The whalebone arch above Whitby,
A giant wishbone above the sea,

Which we could never pull apart,
Dark as old blood, the human heart.

I ran my hands over its surface, glossy
As the wave's silk negligee,

Imagined the harpoon, the cable stretching
A bass string,

At the pitch of death, the deck awash with blood,
The man wearing
A black apron made of whale's skin,

Grins as he holds the knife,
A trophy. Death is the price we pay for life,

Degraded though
The resurrected song drifts through

The sea, until two plumes of water glow.

A cavalier's feather,
An embryonic rainbow.

III

These are the paths where the swineherd Caedmon walked
Above the sea
While he sang to the Lord,

And did it seem as if the Lord answered
With cloud pale and transparent as alabaster,
Effigies of old gods in crumbling steam
Above the horizon,
As he heard the voice of the Lord,
In the famished light of buttercups,
The balance of a gull,
Its screamed signal
Promising blood,
Its mouth scissors, a scythe of bone, a sword?

IV

As Caedmon walked on the headland and listened,
To the boom of the sea,
The scream of the wind,
To the hiss of the waves
Sousing their life away

It seemed that he heard
In the voice of these things
The clash of swords, the English word
That kills as it sings,

The word sung in praise of God,
Who utters the sibilant syllables of the sea
Rank as urine in the byre and warm as cow's blood
But distant too,

As shoals of light where we
Float and break apart
The shadow line of the horizon,
The periphery of the heart.

My Cat and Crazy Rainbows

For Serhij

Your 1972 Lada farts through the park in Lutsk
As you weave around a gum-booted Babusya, two kids
Licking either side of a vanilla cornet in the dusk,

Let the light of Christ enter your heart
The CD you have chosen for me (Po Anhliyske!
Vam spodobayetsya?) rasps as we float

Over the grass a respiring sea,
Your Lada magicked into a boat,
Your mirrored glasses, a pool of mercury,

Reflect my face reflected in the rear view mirror,
A million Steves soundlessly mouthing fuck
As you slalom past a teenage footballer,

Swerve back onto the road and brake
Outside the tax office leaving
A spectral sea of exhaust in your wake.

I could not find anything smaller,
You pressed a dollar into my hand,
A bigger man than me, though I was taller,

And gave me the CD I never listen to,
Though sometimes I flash it in the sunlight
For my cat and crazy rainbows grin like you.

Vasya's Biggest Secret

is the skull,
He brings me wrapped in polythene
I unfold gingerly.
The black hairline cracks over the cranium,
And one oddly neat hole,
A full stop drilled over the right eye socket.
Can a skull look surprised
At its owner's fate?
Vasya swears the man was left unburied in the Steppe grass,
The red dust of Crimea covered him,
The last tenderness he had known,
The dark Eurasian night,
Warm as the Black Sea lapping over his skin.
I wonder if the sound of the sea resides in the skull,
The way the ocean lisps inside a sea shell,
Or is the noise I think I hear
The whisper of a human soul,
The bloodied waves sighing over the shore of Crimea?
I hand it back, my fingers in each eye hole
As if it were a bowling ball.
He folds it carefully back in polythene
And lays it on the spare wheel
Next to a loaf. Closes the boot on its grin.

There Are Mirrors

That reflect not only our image
But other mirrors, where we are also reflected, so
It seems we walk among a collection of ourselves,
Each identical
But subtly different in some way
We can't quite catch and each
With the same smile or bemused look. In Prague
I walked among a maze

With you and felt your hand,
Small and intimate as an anemone
With the sea, in mine,
Fingers, pale fronds sifting the light. From
Behind walls of mirrors and balsa wood
We heard
Human voices,
A dog barking and the city itself
A long sibilant hiss,
Like the wind among birches.

I thought
I held the key in my hand,
The keys that chimed
That day in Wenceslas Square,
As people rang
For freedom to come,
Or at least the choice
To be a partial slave and see
The reflection of your voice
As liberty,

But it was nothing in the end
Except daylight
Stringent as redemption,
Recesses
Of birch and bracken
Where your tongue
Is mine.

Lenin Takes a Dip or the Poem with the Word S*** in it Six Times

A museum of discarded Lenin statues has been opened in the waters off the Crimean Coast.

There is something remorseless
About how the waves brush
The sides of the boat,
And how the heat
Makes Balaclava ripple,
And the distant bluffs unreal,

The headland, a crumbling skull.
I relax and breathe and roll
Backwards to fall,
Wriggle then balance.
Silence. A Black Sea Bass
Gives me a blank glance,

Its eyes are buttons, buttons
Of polished jet, the dorsal spines
Needles of black bone.
It's got rhythm, man.
Five beats and it's gone.
I kick my way down

To the bed. Deep blue light.
Scarves of weed undulate.
I move slowly. The water's weight
Makes time dilate,
And sound radiate.
Your wordless shout

Surrounds me slowly as you drift,
Back heel pearls and lift
A couple of feet
To where the white
Bust of Lenin stares
Through the coastal waters.

His eyes blank as two ducks' eggs.
His wordless gaze begs,
Or seems to beg.
I've got him pegged,
With an old quote
That bubbles towards the boat,

"What is Russia? Russia is shit,"
He said once, "shit, Honvo,"
And his glance is shit too
Shit or bad art.
We dance in the dark light
Around him with linked arms

And celebrate all the shit things.
Even a murderer's statue has its charms.

Khersonesos

For SJS

I dreamed we were asleep at Khersonesos
Under the stars between the broken pillars
Of what once was the Temple of Artemis,
Your head was lain upon my breast,
And your forehead was the colour of the moon
And your hand, swift as a lizard, ran
Through the scree and grass of Ai Petri,
And your eyes were the mountain flowers
Gathered on my breast at Khersonesos
And Homer's wine dark sea and loss.

Pavlo's Lament

After Tychyna

I

In the replay of our last embrace
Your mouth moves towards mine,
In some well-lit, soundless place
Where desires happen,

But at the last moment you slip
Away from me and disintegrate
Into the shadows of the Steppe.
The noiseless movement of wheat.

II

Spring in the flex of an elm's branch
Or the chance
Dimple of water
Where the river shapes to sand and stone
Or scampers through itself laughing.

III

Summer in the blonde or the bronze surf
Of rye,
At midday or at dusk
As you walk by. One of the stalks perhaps
Plucked like an eyelash.

IV

Autumn comes bereft of love,
The half-formed human
Shapes of fog,
A blurred wave,
A dagger in a silk glove.

V

Snowflakes partner and dance
Into a kind of death,
While the wind laments them
With its almost human breath.

Too supple to hold,
You elude me, leaving my arms
Empty and cold. Soft feathers on my face,
With a touch difficult as love or chance.

All our voices lost
In a huge silence.

Cathedral

After Tychyna

The dexterous curve of a willow,
Flighted towards the earth,
Casts a net
Over the path
By a melon, to whose droll
Rotundity and leaf parasol,
The sun is an obsessive thought.
The green hymn of this place
Calls on us, with its wordless
Invocation, to arise
With our tiny deities,
The camellia waves farewell,
And quietly, again
I hear the earth exhale
A living organ.

Nowhere

there are times you just want to drive or walk
nowhere – the place that everyone has been to
but is marked on no maps   and starting
the car or stepping out of the door
you follow your intuition to the end of the road
taking a right or a left
pausing to admire a cloudscape
the movement of light on the river

and these events cohere into a narrative
that does not differ from the story
you were telling yourself anyway
even in the silence when you looked in the mirror
at the face you have worn
which at that moment you are most alone
feels alien but familial a stranger
you have grown comfortable with

walking with you in footsteps not your own
or driving past
industrial estates at the edge of town
or stepping into the forest
offering the illusion of paths
a Gordian knot of infinitely looped possibilities
among flattened grass
snapped twigs

but only now you realise
the only way to arrive at nowhere
is to forget that you are travelling
and it happens suddenly
the steps coming to a halt

the bicycle slanted on the five bar gate
the car pulled over in a layby
a car park   grass   hills   tree

the derelict factory
or church   the house
whose door you open
the stile where you sit
the car with the engine cooling
the darkness where you settle
knowing that whatever you look at
nowhere is as beautiful

as nowhere

I Dreamed

I dreamed you knitted me the River Colne
In silk shot through with blue and grey,
It spilled from your needles of carved bone,
And sighed through the valley,

And you were a birch tree in my arms,
And the sound of my loss was the sound of dogs,
Barking on rusted chains in a thousand farms,
And my arms were severed logs,

But I knew that we would meet,
In the river's backwash, its kiss of foam,
If only as the plaited light,
Sighing as it yearns upwards, home.

Something Fishy

You ran up to me in the recreation ground,
A live carp in your hand,
Its eye
Held a perfectly executed cameo
Of grey Yorkshire sky,
Our two goggling faces
And the gable end of a council semi.

We put him in an old biscuit tin.
Whichever way he turned,
Fish swam
In the same direction
And always came face to face
With a reflection
Of a reflection…

It was a bit of a walk to the old mill pond.
Just for a second
He fell through the air,
A ribbon of fire
Twisting through summer,
A glass crown
On the water.

This Is

My father's cap that often left
A circular dent in his hair, the imprint of a halo
Perhaps, or a circular furrow,

The furrow he ploughed in his father's field
Before the war and exile.
The furrow ploughed by his father,

And if you strung them all together
These furrows would have circled
The world, as they circle it now.

The cap in my hands, a pool
Of time I look down into,
To see my father at the plough

In the sepia light of the thirties,
Lacquered with sweat,
The blade cutting into the fecund dirt,

The oxen stumbling over clods,
My father looking beyond them
To where the earth curves to a cap

Through miles of chocolate corduroy.
His smile flickers briefly,
A kestrel's wingbeat

One shadow rumpling a parachute.

Out of the Belfry

I see your silhouette
Execute a handbrake turn
In mid air at twilight,
Then we watch you perform
My small, mad virtuoso

For nearly twenty minutes,
Your aerobatic solo
In the glow of neon lights
Or through the rectangle
Of vapid luminescence

Thrown onto the gravel
From our window. You hang
Briefly and then you fall,
Looping through a bass clef,
Poise briefly and wobble,

Float up, drop and serve
Yourself like a tennis ball.
Your inaudible squeals
Make blindness visible,
You spin wheels within wheels

Then zip yourself away,
Leaving an absence
In our patch of sky,
A stillness, I feel balance
Between us and Pewle Hill,

A bat outside the belfry
You will fold away
Somewhere into your sleep,
Half mouse, half umbrella.
The scribbled crap I keep.

Too Late

For YK

In the photograph my grandmother is lain

In her coffin. The skin has sagged
Softly in
Between her mouth, nose and chin,
And drawn tight around her forehead.
I never met her

So this picture in a way is a thing,
A thing without any meaning,
As blank as
The dimpled surface of the snow,
In which the coffin is laid,
As fragile and empty

As her withered body. Empty facts too.
She was imprisoned in Vorkuta,
Where she worked
As slave labour
And then lay down to sleep
In wooden barracks

Without heat. She died in eighty-eight,
Still exiled by a government,
Guilty
Of being innocent,
Punished for the crime,
Of living in the wrong place and the wrong time.

Change came, as it always comes,

Late, difficult, uncertain.
Let it seep,
Gently into her skeleton,
And let her sleep begin to warm
With dreams, a tentative

Cyrillic dawn.

Wharncliffe

I

So, the wind grabs
A carrier bag
And inflates it,
To be whisked
        Through a loop and then
        An Immelmann turn
        And surely every knot
        In the repertoire of a boy scout.
To let it drop
And lay
On the grass,
Still bloated
        With air,
        It sways
        In wait
        For a lift,
Its emptiness, my gift.

II

There hasn't been any work
Since the pit closed,
The cranberries whisper.
        Sit and smoke a fag
        Or pick your nose,
        Watch TV, shag,
Have a tattoo,
Buy some clothes,
See the grass sag
        Over the empty mine,

                        A barely noticeable dip
                        In the green satin.
See a crack run
Up your house, a black
Zig zag between the bricks.
Sell your soul old dog, learn
                        New tricks.

III

Summer betrayed us,
Its promise
Dank in the tears
                        Of the couch grass,
                        The inane
                        Lament of a birch
And vacuous mime
Of cirrus
Cloud
                        Its horse hair
                        Its burning sword. This
                        Is the death of things,
This absence,
Implicit
In the blank
Soil, God.

I Did Not Know

That I would let you go
As the river flared over the weir,
Into a row of perspex pillars,

A sneer,
The noise of pummelled water…
You died elsewhere

Alone, below a magnolia ceiling,
Perhaps catching the last whiff of spring,
Through the opened window

Sunlight laid a gold javelin
Across your breast.
At last

All that you could not know…
Every state is a protection racket
You said

From within your cumulous cloud
Of tobacco smoke, its copperplate
Flourishes, its scrolls, its silk,

The police protect the wolves from the sheep,
Your cupped hand glowed orange
In the glow of your pipe.

You died while I looked
At the River Colne,
And the river breathed,

A black ribbon, the reflection
Of birches
Broken. Gone.

Vasya's Surprise

I

I followed you, stumbling over the tussocks with my five year old's feet, while you swished at dandelion clocks in the fallow pasture with the ebony walking stick considered by some a dandyish affectation. The water spattering into the tin bath. Once, when I was praying to the brass Christ that hung over my bed, he shook his head slightly as if refusing my prayers. I turned off the light to hide from his face, but it was your face I saw absurdly hovering in the dark disembodied like the moon. I tried to speak but the words turned to iron and fell out of my mouth as wing nuts, a bolt, drill bits.

II

The shell had crashed through the thatch in nineteen-fifteen and failed to explode. Now it lay its brass muzzle resting on a beam, angled like a seal diving. Forever frozen in mid flight, its tail fins caught and held in the straw of the roof. It had hung over your bed for ten years, invisible above the lacquered wood of the ceiling. As you fell asleep, sometimes you thought of the shadow of death hanging over you or wondered when your father would return from Gdansk, his visits now so remote that he seemed alien in his patent leather shoes, shiny as a cockroach shell, his hair lacquered into place, and a pair of wire-rimmed pince-nez. There was a point when you hated him, but now he is merely a stranger who talks to you of the joys of flying and how one day you will soar like an eagle over the Baltic. He brings your mother an amber pendant like an ochre tear, but her eyes remain glazed and shiny as his hands fasten the clasp of the chain behind her neck and he kisses the top of her head gently. He leaves the next day before dawn, you hear his Praga Piccolo car start into life with a noise that still sounds strange and alien. You think of its radiator grille like the smile on a Greek comedic mask. Your cat, Franz, named after the Austro-Hungarian Emperor, purrs under the bed like a finely tuned motor. As you go back to sleep you dream of bees, of running water.

III

You cross a plank bridge, which hangs from wooden posts on gently sagging ropes over the water, to get to the church. There are gaps between the wood on which you step, through which you see the surface of the river, opaque and brown, sometimes glimmering with sunlight, monstrous and robed in a subtle garment of silk. Sometimes the bridge sways and tilts so you find yourself hanging on, face to face with a death that resembles yourself, your reflection breaking and coagulating like globules of mercury. You look away and see a small, black bull eyeing you curiously with what seems to be a state of recognition before swishing its tail dismissively, then you swing still higher and see the sky and then see the water again.

Vasya grabs your arm when you get to the other side and drags you through a clump of bushes to where the graves of a cemetery used by the colonists are gradually disappearing under weeds and grass. He and his friends have lifted the massive stone slab to one side to reveal the dark corpse of a man in the stone catacomb underneath, wearing a shroud that resembles a nighty. Strangely he is not laid out flat but has been moved into a sitting position with a chair improvised from whatever stones came to hand, a kind of small cairn really. His blank eye sockets stare up at you. Feeling sick you force a smile, even pat Vasya on the back. Well done.

IV

The lake steps with blue tears, while above the sky says, do not weep, but it may not stop the grieving of the waters, cloud after cloud tearing the spirit.

Geese, white as snow, on the banks, geese whose wings murmur in the air like the soft feathered fall of snow, why do you not hold the gale back? So the orchard stands in the depths of the valley, sensing the autumn in its perpetual song, so the wind scampers to the walnut trees, so the trees let their yellowed notes fall, forgetting to sing soaring to the acacia, so the acacia hastens too much, and the voice of the wind in the weeds whispers and I? and I? And disperses. So you are not willing to sing! Already it passes beyond the village, beyond November and its last phrase glimmers, circle, spheres! And the weed's voice follows, yearning to be soft, tender as a dove's breast.

The lake steps with blue tears. And only the alternate wave stipples things with time like sand. The rust coloured shore light blurred as with dove feathers the geese...

Monet

I

Branch of the Seine near Vetheuil 1878

Camille Monet on her deathbed 1879

Covered by a membrane
Of indigo and silver light,
The surface of the Seine
Reflects explosions of shrubs at sunset.

You have painted the moment itself
When shapes disintegrate,
The spire of a poplar prominent
Against cloud, local yet displaced,

Petering out at the edges
Into the summer of Vetheuil,
Echoing the transparencies
Over Camille,

The face of a woman asleep through a veil
Of gauze perhaps. I do not know
How, through your grief, you control
The ephemeral glow

Of perception, eternal
In the miracle that makes colours move,
Blur, shift, and live. The pool
Of light on each canvas. Smeared love.

II

The sun itself

What made you think of it
The sun, bright and definite
As a clementine
Where the turquoise light
Blurs through mauve, pink and yellow
Over the Seine?
What I most admire
Is how you catch the water
And the way that shapes
Collide through each other,
Or the way a tree spills through
Sky and absorbs it too,

And how boats and people
Appear through a few simple
Strokes of darker blue,
The clinging and supple
Reflection of shrubbery
Falling away

Into a world beyond
Canvas or oil, a hand
Momentarily,
Lifted and balanced,
In the brief buoyancy

Where we are free

To become the space
That colours play.

III

Fishermen at Poissy 1882

Those anglers at Poissy are more detailed
Than your usual people, painted at an angle,
So the whole scene is killed to the side
And it seems the river and boats will spill

Through the corner into the world, except
For the green and brown diagonal
And triangle of path and grass that wedged
The river in its place and made it real,

As real as those poplars implicit,
In the pillars of spilled green light,
Implied but not painted, and the weight
Of those rods angled from the boat

And the chime of water. Feel it. Float.

What?

It is not the moment which you inhabit at this second
Nor the moments you abandoned,
Or indeed the act of forgetting in itself,
The recognition
That a face is familiar

But also unknown, though it drifts occasionally
In your sleep, the balloon
Left behind after a party, and the features
Themselves loose distinction
Until it is the echo of a face,

A few cursory strokes that remind you
Of the chance dialogue
Between two seemingly unrelated objects.
No, nor is it the time
When you feel the greatest intimacy with the city

In the half light in its unfinished places, the sites
Which you sense will remain half built,
A section of wall, here the first
Tentative probings of dock and nettle and the neon lights
A mere suggestion

Of clarity. You will remember not what you saw
As a child, but what you saw
Afterwards, the branch
Left empty by a kingfisher swinging
Not as if it were saying goodbye

But saying nothing really, the silence
Filled with noise you never listen to,
Your voice saying something
Even now you don't catch.

A Quail Flies Over the Steppe,
From an old Cossack ballad

So no cuckoo cooed and no bird
Sang in the orchard,
Though the maiden called
Her brother home.

Brother, I beseech you,
Swim the river,
As a white swan,
Fly over the wide Steppe

As a quail,
Cross over the dark meadow,
As a hawk,
Alight

As a dove
At my door
Murmuring
Sorrowfully.

Sister take
A pinch of yellow sand,
Sow it on the white stone.
Make a cross of flowers

With blooms white
As dove feathers.
Then I will come
To you again.

The Zone
for Sohail Khan

It's a kick up the arse wind
Funnelling down the Colne Valley,
Whipping the birch trees,
Orchestrated frenzy

                              Time lapse cirrus cloud,
                              Horse hair or perhaps
                              Candy floss, a shroud,
                              A divot of foam

Dug out of the river,
Drifts upwards, yearning home,
Couch grass garrottes everything.
Oh, my yellow assassin

                    Your roots snake,
                    And grip my mouth,
                    I slither down the stones of the bank
                    And follow the river

To the ugly south.

***

Burdock proffers its green tongue,
The thistle sings its lightning,
The first bud proffers a sword tip
To fend off sleep,

                          I watch the creep of light
                          Among birch trees bronze
                          Shifts through indigo, violet
                          The night, hieroglyphic

Let me read it with my skin,
The touch
Of birch silken,
The lush scent

                        Of this spring,
                        A sin.
                        In the black cocoon,
                        Let me be part of the mindless

Kingdom of green
And my heart sing.

***

There's bugger all here
Except a crow planting
Both feet firmly in the air
As it takes off.

                        The droll
                        Rotundity of a tennis ball,
                        Loosing its covering
                        And revealing its rubber soul,

You exhale
A plume of smoke,
It unravels and blows east,
A cavalier's ghost

                        And birches
                        Break into a dance,
                        A punchline
                        Searching for a joke

As you roam the waste ground
To get lost. To be found.

***

A rusted hub cap
Hangs from an elm tree,
An excremental sun
Whispers for me

                                          Your island is full
                                          Of ugly noises,
                                          The plash of a mallard,
                                          The river's spitterish lisp

You weave wool around tree trunks,
Psychedelic spider's web,
Making art from what you find,
The heart beats blindly

                              In two-four time
                              Reaching the end of the line,
                              Tall, rangy as a heron,
                              You sift among bindweed and slime,
This rubbish, all you could wish for, abandoning
Yourself to the crime of life, the river's delirious swing.

***

August Moon

For SJS

who has not watched the full moon in August?
orange and pumpkin plump, against a sky lilac
or violet shifting through indigo, on the horizon
over the gentle slope of a sand dune or a city scape,
hearing the wind boom through the trees
or the soft static of summer rain or traffic

and known that someone must watch,
as you are watching now, the slow levitation
of the moon over the edge of things,
a Chinese lantern buoyed in the dark
by the weak fire whispering inside,
and who has not felt the world recede,

and heard the call of a world
beyond the world we inhabit, a world
of other worlds, infinite, and called
to whoever happens to be standing by
look at the moon, look and pointed
to the moon, and beyond it the sky,

but really looking at the candle inside
its flame seemingly weak, its waxy tears
soft as August rain upon your skin,
its light, pathetic and about to expire
but strong enough to illuminate
the moon, and everything beyond it?

From Edinburgh

I

The wind swirls leaves
Up Princess Street
Partners,
A crisp packet
      In a spastic tango,
      Edinburgh grieves,
      Mid day autumnal light
      Softening the shades of granite
To a grey arpeggio.
A face glimpsed through a car window,
Pale and somehow Irish,
The dreams where the dead speak
      Noiselessly as fish
      In the aquarium light
      Above Arthur's seat.
      The hand
Almost tenderly
Releasing your throat.

II

You might come across him
At twilight, daft Jamie
Invisibly
Passing by,
      Wave him a shroud
      Of bladderwrack and cloud,
      His turf a sod,
      His blood,

The rain running down
The castle walls,
The boy's last sigh
As he falls,
                      Among the tide
                      Shucking razor shells
                      A sail bellies,
                      In Forth and Cromarty,
Albion cries
Butchered by the lines
Of human geography.
The sea. And then the sea.

III

He lays on the table dead,
As only the dead are able,
Butcher boy Knox looms over him
With apron and scalpel
                      And slices a line
                      Above his hips and through his navel,
                      As Albion is severed
                      By Hadrian's Wall,
The blade seems gentle,
A ship's keel off Finisterre,
That's Jamie,
Whispers,
                      A shadow on the granite stair,
                      A trick of the light,
                      Breath evaporating from a mirror,
                      Basalt.

The sea line dances in
Waves recoil off the jetty
Not quite Doopsie Doing
In not quite four-four time.

IV

Though I walk
By the waters of Leith,
This river will not forget,
Or grieve,

                        As it flows over the weir,
                        Sheer as a silk stocking,
                        The wind among the trees
                        Sets them rocking,

I fall at your knees
In repentance,
My head knocking you gently,
A boat at a quay,

                        The river exiles itself
                        Down the incline
                        Of a coastal shelf,
                        Though for us this dawn

All the birds sing
From the Hebrides to Devon,
Music in different keys

Their mickle song.

I Loved to Walk Around the Cages at Night,

Though I was barely tall enough to peek over the floor
Of the trailer and between the bars
I loved the reek of animals and straw,
The grass under my feet, the summer stars.

The zebras seemed little more than the reflection
Of branches and moonlight upon the water,
The lion might have been chiseled from stone,
The tiger coalesced and dispersed like quicksilver.

Once I heard two men walking towards me
Speaking a language I didn't know,
I ducked between the trailers and waited only to see
My father materialise from the shadow

By the largest cage where the elephants slept
And a man who might have been my uncle,
The chief clown, who was particularly adept
With balloons and had once fashioned a poodle

For me as an especial gift, though he was a hard man
With a convict's pale musculature,
And stars and onion domes tattooed on his skin,
And of course the Mother of God

Aureoled with ink-stylised clouds cherubim
And her rather smug looking son.
My father seemed to be talking Ukrainian
The language my Danish mother had forbidden,

What use is it Leonid? she had said.
Near them on the grass a sack stirred,
A goose pilfered from some nearby farm
Still living though its neck was broken.

A Letter from Crimea

For Vyacheslav Huk

I would have written on a Cypress leaf,
Or doodled my letter in Turkic on the sand
With a Kukri knife,
At dusk the trees converse among themselves,
The Black Sea sighs on the beach,
As if trying to say the words
I grope for and cannot reach.

There are no pens here,
The timbers of the barracks sigh at night,
I wonder if this is Europe's heart,
While the window lays a sharp sign on the floor.
I peer through glass at waves that slide
Through the Cyrillic alphabet,
A cursive script of shadow and foam
All that remains unspoken,
The painted eyes of triremes, yearning home.

Translations

The poem overleaf was written by Volymyr Svidzinskyi (1885-1941) in 1934 and is, in my view, the greatest poem written by any soviet poet in the Stalinist period. I make that assertion not because the poem is technically innovative but because it exemplifies what Keats called negative capability. Svidzinskyi will have seen the results of Stalin's policies in Ukraine, but he does not moralise, condemn or posture. He simply conveys the effect on him, and therefore on anyone whose conscience was not poisoned by the party's slogans, of what he experienced. He would later be burned alive by the NKVD, but the poem speaks as clearly to us now as it did then to those people who passed it from hand to hand. The poem's genius is that it says everything by saying nothing, and the poet's courage in facing both a hopeless situation and its deadening effect on him is inspirational. The English version is not literal but I believe it captures the essence of the poem, for I know that it is the lustre of the surface and not the gleam of the mirror that is important.

"Лице люстра мертвіє в тіні..."

Лице люстра мертвіє в тіні
І задавнена тиша спить,
Як налита в миску вода.
Тільки руки мої живуть -
Іноді чудно, якось окремо,
Іноді рух моїх рук
Вертає мене з задуми,
Як шурхіт у легкому листі.
Я встаю, іду до вікна.
Надбита колонка стоїть коло ґанку,
Цвіль у її жолобках.
Долітають сюди сніжечки,
Долітають синиці ранками.
Прихилюся чолом до скла,
Довго на них дивлюсь.
Не люблю, як приходить ніч,
Завинена в темний платок
З імшано-зеленим цвітом.
Тиша стікає в великий став.
Сині синиці, де ви вночі?
Лице люстра трупіє в тіні,
Завіси стають кам'яні,
І, обчеркнений колом мовчання,
Я глухіше, сумніше горю,
Я горю, як китайський ліхтарик,
Забутий на гілці, в старому саду.

The Lustre of Surfaces

The lustre of surfaces dies into the shadow
And antique silence sleeps,
Like water decanted into a bowl.
Only my hands live,
Strange and separate,
Their movements
Compel me to meditate,
Like the whisper of a leaf.
I go to the window,
A broken post stands by the verandah,
Mould grows in the guttering
Where snowflakes gather in winter,
Where birds alight in the morning.
I press my forehead against the glass
And gaze for a while.
I don't love the advent of night
It seems guilty, a dark linen,
The blurred green edges of vegetation.
A huge pool of silence accumulates.
Where have the birds gone?
The lustrous surface of things dies,
The curtains hang motionless
As if carved in stone.
In my defined circle of silence
I become more insensitive, and sad,
As a forgotten, Chinese lantern caught
On a branch in some old orchard.

Bohdan Ihor Antonych (1909-1937) took the folklore language and traditions of the Lemky region, which was part of Poland between the first and second world wars, and transplanted them into literary Ukrainian. The Lemky were a Ukrainian mountain people whose culture and traditions were rooted in crop cycles and pagan mythology, and in Antonych's work the boundaries between the narrator, the natural world and the music of the poems become blurred within an ecstatic pagan celebration of life.

The ethnic community in which Antonych's language was rooted would be destroyed after the war when, during a brutal exercise termed "Operation Vistula", the Lemky were deported from their homeland in order to crush the Ukrainian underground and resettled elsewhere in Poland (http://en.wikipedia.org/wiki/Operation_Vistula#Deportations_and_repressions). There is still an active Lemky Ukrainian community, but the organic connection to the soil has been broken and with it the variant of Ukrainian spoken by Antonych only exists like a specimen preserved in formaldehyde. However, the paganism of his poetry and the celebration in this poem of a transcendent love are conveyed in a language that seems effortlessly ecstatic and achieved.

Дует

Поволі повертаємось у землю, як в колиску,
вузли зелені зілля в'яжуть нас — два сплутані акорди.
Сокира сонця вбита в пень дубовий лезом блиску,
музика моху, ласка вітру, дуб, мов ідол, гордий.

На тратві дня, що нас несе, тіла слухняні й теплі
зростаються з собою, мов два сни, два вірні квіти.
Мов шерсть кота, нас гріє мох. Заміниш зорі в шепіт,
заміниш кров у зелень і музику. Небо світить.

Де берег дня, за морем неба, сплять вітри майбутні
і наші вірні зорі — наші долі ждуть в заморях,
поки не здійсняться з землі наказу. В се несутнє
відкинемо і лиш екстазу чисту візьмем зорям.

Болить натхнення крові. Брови, мов дві стріли, колють,
і мур мелодії над нами, мов луна велика,
немов крило вітрів. Від зір залежить наша доля.
Гориш рослинна й спрагла, мов земля. Ти вся музика.

Duet

We return slowly to the earth, our cradle.
Green tangles of vegetation bind us, two fettered chords.
The razor sharp axe of sun hews at a trunk,
The music of moss, tenderness of the breeze, the oak a proud
                                                                                idol.

In the wastage of days that bear us the body, warm and
                                                                             obedient
Grows with itself, two siblings, two flowers of fidelity.
The moss warms us like cat fur. You transform the stars into a
                                                                      murmur
And blood into music and greenery. The sky glows.

At the edge of day, in the ocean of heaven, the winds of the
                                                                      future sleep
And our devoted constellations wait under the frost,
While earth does not instruct them to arise. We abandon
                                                                        things,
To be borne, to grasp the stars in pure ecstasy.

The yearning of blood hurts. Eyebrows sharp as two arrows,
While above us a wall of melody echoes
The pinions of a breeze. Our fate pinned on the planets.
You burn with growth, thirsty as the earth. Become all music.

www.ingramcontent.com/pod-product-compliance
Lightning Source LLC
Chambersburg PA
CBHW052134010526
44113CB00036B/2257